ALLEZ!

published by

Cookie Jar Publishing
332 W. Martin Lane, Salt Lake City, Utah 84107 U.S.A.
www.CookieJarPublishing.com

Carson-Dellosa Publishing Co., Inc.
7027 Albert Pick Road, Greensboro, NC 27409 U.S.A.
www.CarsonDellosa.com

ISBN 1-59441-498-x

Book Design, Project Management and Production by George Starks and Dante Orazzi

Second Printing, July 2005

10 9 8 7 6 5 4 3 2

Mike and the Bike

Written by Michael Ward ✦ Illustrated by Bob Thomson ✦ Foreword by Lance Armstrong

COOKIE JAR PUBLISHING

For

Tennessee, Seth, Sophie,
Bella, Grace, and Luke

I have been a musician most of my life. I took up the guitar at the age of ten, encouraged and supported every step of the way by my loving parents. I did not, however, discover cycling until my mid-twenties, when I was looking for a way to get in shape and enjoy the great outdoors. Well, I certainly found what I was looking for! Riding the bike has become as important and fulfilling for me as anything I have ever known. Every ride is an adventure, and cycling has changed my life in ways I never thought possible.

This book is my humble offering to anyone who loves bikes, children, music, and any combination thereof! Sharing music and cycling with my son Tennessee has been endlessly rewarding to me, and we are happy to share Mike and the Bike with you.

Enjoy the book and music, and get on your bikes and ride!

Michael Ward
Los Angeles, CA

At a very young age I fell in love with my bike—and not much has changed!
I have ridden thousands and thousands of miles around the world.
I have made friends from all walks of life.
And I have learned that many times in life the things that we enjoy
most as children are the things that we turn to and enjoy the most
throughout our entire lives!

To me, there really is nothing like riding a bike,
and I am excited to introduce you to someone who reminds me
a lot of myself—his name is Mike!

I think that you will like reading and riding with Mike,
so when you are done, hop on, go for a ride, and have some fun!

Enjoy the Ride!

LANCE ARMSTRONG

This is a boy whose name is **Mike.**

MIKE

Puzzles, games, and . . .
. . . big . . . bouncing . . . balls . . .

Faraway Places get closer, you see...

Point

When riding your bike from point **A** ----> to point **B**.

When a long day of riding
has come to an end,
Mike and the bike
head back home
once again.

Home

Mike cleans the bike, and he puts it away.

And dreams of the next ride the very next day.

Victory Lap!

Tennessee Rides!

Phil and Michael at the Tour.

Michael and Lance
Photo Credit: www.kreutzphotography.com

Michael Wins!
(What he won and where he is, no one knows.)

George in Peru!!

Victory in Sight!

★ Enjoy ★ the Ride!

Rock'n & Roll'n with Tennessee!

Michael Rides the Glandon!

Lance and Michael on Big T!
Photo Credit: Mark Higgins

Michael Rides the Madeleine

Going for It!

Dante, left, and Friends Bike Moab!

Lance Narrates Mike and the Bike Foreword!

Tennessee Wins! (beating his Dad with ease)

Mike and the Bike

Mike and the Bike
Mike and the Bike
Riding around doing what they like
Mike and the Bike
Mike and the Bike
Let's take a ride with Mike and the Bike

Rollin'

We're rollin'
We're rollin'
We're rollin' on down the road
We're rollin'
We're rollin'
Gonna roll all the way back home

Wake up in the morning
We hit the streets
Hold on to the handlebars
Pedal with our two feet

We climb up the hills
And then we come back down
Like a spirit in the wind
The wheels keep turnin' 'round

Sing Along with Mike!

I Want To Ride

I want to ride
I want to ride on my bike
It's a feeling that I like
I want to ride

I want to ride down the street
Oh, the people I will meet
I want to ride

I want to ride all day long
As I sing my cycling song
I want to ride

And when I ride the whole day through
You know I'm riding straight to you

I want to ride

I want to ride to my school
I am such a riding fool
I want to ride

I want to ride home with you
What a lovely thing to do
I want to ride

And when we ride into the night
Nothing else could ever feel so right

I want to ride

Pedal Power

Pedal power
Every hour
Pedal power
Every hour

movin' and groovin'
ridin' and flyin'
livin' and spinnin'
laughin', not cryin'

Pedal power
Every hour
Pedal power
Sweet and sour

wheelin' and feelin'
shiftin' and liftin'
goin' and flowin'
showin' and mowin'
eatin' and sleepin'
rockin' and rollin'
spinnin' and grinnin' and winnin'...

Pedal power
Every hour
Pedal power
Pick some flowers
Pedal power
Every hour
Pedal power
Take a shower...

Excuse Me Sir

Excuse me, Sir, but I just might
have a flat tire on my bike.
If you'd be so kind to help me out,
that's what sharing is all about.

Excuse me, Miss, if you could please
help me with the scrape on my knees.
I've just fallen off my bike;
I'll be your friend, my name is Mike.
Thank you!

This book could not have been made without major help and enthusiasm from the following people:
James Achor, Lance Armstrong, Janet and Bill Bradley, Baxter Brings, Tim Cadiente, Bill Cass, Bryan Christner,
Dan Cross, Tom DeSavia, Tracy and Chad Hartfiel, Russ Hymas, Bart Knaggs, John Korioth, Elizabeth Kreutz,
Dante Orazzi, Terri Phillips, Gary and Shirlee Phillips, Julian Raymond, Curt Schneider, Bill Stapleton, George Starks,
Bob Thomson, Richard R. Ward, Rich, Kaitlyn, and Kiersten Ward, and, of course, Tennessee.

Michael Ward
★ ★

Bob would like to thank:
Maryann - I couldn't have done this without your help and support, Seth - for being so patient,
The Warden, George Starks, and Dante Orazzi.

Bob Thomson
★ ★

Thanks to Mom, Dad, Michael, Anne, and everyone at Orazzi's Blue Ridge Inn.
Thanks to Dawna, Slim, Skyler & Mikaela Simmons for fighting the fight and "Living Strong!"
Thanks to George Starks, Baxter Brings, Steve Carson, Tom Hall, Danell & Kyle, James Morris, Z&C, Meradyth,
Gil Ruiz, Canty, Kowalczyk, Ruddy, McDonnell, Bart, Lucy, Toni, Alex, and to HP for being a great friend.

Dante Orazzi
★ ★

There are so many people to thank for putting up with me and my constant state of motion, but Mom and Dad you are
at the top of the list! Scott, my best friend, thanks for leading me to Mike and the Bike. Kelly, Jason, Megan, Mary,
Michael, and Shayneh, Ryan, and Dave, I wish all of you the best ride life has to offer. Fonda, your wisdom helped pedal
Mike across the finish line, and of course Steve and Baxter, thank you for believing in me, and this project. Danell, there is
no way to thank you enough, James, Robyn, Andy, Kristy, Amanda, Paul and Magen—thank you for showing up to work
every day and motivating me to get on the next flight! Tim, Dan, Sara, Brent, Greg, Elvis, Freddie, J-Juip, Jason, Louie,
Kathleen, Rebecca, Dave, Debbie, Tessa, and above all, Vanessa (Blue Star) thank you for supporting, inspiring and
consoling me each day in your own way to continue searching and believing in myself, and others.

George Starks
★ ★